Capsized in the Solent

The *SRN6-012* Hovercraft Disaster

Richard M. Jones

ISBN: 978-1-326-58484-9

First published in Great Britain in 2016 by

Lodge Books
25 South Back Lane
Bridlington
www.lodgebooks.co.uk

About the author

Richard M. Jones has been researching disasters, especially shipwrecks, his whole life. His previous books have seen previously unknown stories brought to light as well as plaques installed for those without a permanent memorial. A serving member of the Royal Navy, he spends his time between Bridlington and Southampton and always has a project ongoing.

By the same author

The Great Gale of 1871
Lockington – Crash at the Crossing
The Burton Agnes Disaster
End of the Line – The Moorgate Disaster

This book is dedicated to all those who risk their lives at sea to rescue others.

Contents

Introduction

As a man who has spent his entire life studying disasters around the world that have been forgotten, I thought I had seen pretty much every kind of tragedy and freak accident over the years. Countless books tell stories of human suffering in the most unheard of ways – a coal tip covering a school, a fighter jet cutting the high wire holding a cable car, and even an explosion which happened weeks after a train crash on the same spot caused by repair vehicles hitting a gas pipe. But in 1997 I found an article that had me looking at a disaster that I had not only never heard of but one I would never have thought possible – the capsizing of a hovercraft. It was a copy of the Daily Mail, and buried at the back of the newspaper was a small section that gives you a run through of what happened 'on this day'; in this case it was the twenty-fifth anniversary of the capsizing of such a craft off Southsea, Hampshire, which led to several passenger deaths.

Now reading things like this doesn't usually shock me, but what does shock me is that even today nobody has ever heard of this tragedy, unless they have a particular interest in hovercraft or were actually there at the time. It was years later, after I had placed memorials to several other forgotten disasters, that I thought I would make an effort to highlight this incident by writing a book about it and if possible installing a plaque somewhere nearby to remember the five people who had died that day.

This is where I found it more difficult than I could have imagined. People didn't remember it; those who survived were from all around the world (very few it seemed from the local area); very little reporting was done on it; and the libraries and archives pretty much drew a blank. Starting with the newspapers from the day I worked my way through history, which took me years of collecting reports, news articles and the odd few eyewitness accounts, but today this is my best attempt at telling the story of the capsizing of the Southsea hovercraft *SRN6-012*.

Make no mistake, it has taken a lot of courage for people to open up about such a traumatic event, from the people who witnessed the capsizing to those who had to deal with the victims. For this I thank them in their efforts and hope that I have put their stories in a way that does them justice.

This is not the first time I have written about forgotten disasters and most likely won't be the last. I have so far put up five memorial plaques for disasters such as the Moorgate tube crash of 1975 and written four other books to date, telling stories that have never before seen the light of day. The research into the Southsea hovercraft disaster took me over six years to compile. Hopefully now it will never be forgotten to history.

1. The floating aircraft

Southsea is a part of Portsmouth that has been popular with holidaymakers since anyone could remember. The beaches look out onto the body of water known as the Solent and in the distance you can clearly see the Isle of Wight, with ferries running regularly for those wanting to go over for a day trip, holiday or work. The crowds at the Southsea beach will notice many attractions such as Southsea Castle where Henry VIII watched his favourite warship *Mary Rose* sink in 1545 with the loss of up to 700 crew. That area of water, although small, has seen its fair share of shipwrecks over the years. As well as the *Mary Rose* the seabed around the Isle of Wight is littered with historic warships such as the *Royal George* and *Invincible*, a troopship called the *Mendi* and several submarines. Ships have plied these waters for centuries and today is no different, with more shipping movements than ever as ships get bigger and holidays get cheaper.

Ask anybody who is stood watching from the seafront at Southsea to point to all the different types of ship they see and you will get the standard answers – warships, ferries, maybe a cruise liner, and plenty of car and cargo carriers. But one craft that you are guaranteed to look upon several times a day is the hovercraft that usually runs from Southsea beach to Ryde on the Isle of Wight. The hovercraft is a special class of its own because in technical terms they are not defined as a ship – they actually come under aviation. This is due to them gliding across the waves on an inflatable air bag, with the propeller at the rear pushing the salty air through its huge blades causing the kinetic energy to build and therefore giving the hovercraft its 'lift' and sending it on its way on what is known as a 'flight' across the water, the captain being known as the pilot. It was an argument that stemmed from the fact that the hovercraft was neither a ship nor an aircraft; it was simply classed as 'hovercraft', in its own category, after the Hovercraft Act was passed placing operational control with the Marine Department but with certification from the Air Registration Bureau.

3

The story of the hovercraft begins really just after the Second World War when designs were put forward for a new type of seagoing vessel. The first real fully built hovercraft were tested and in service by the end of the 1950s, and ready for the general public to use as a ferry across such waters as the English Channel and Solent by the early 1960s. It was here that the company Hovertravel was founded in 1965 to provide a fast and efficient service taking around three dozen passengers at any one time to the Isle and back. This gave passengers a very quick way of reaching the island as well as the novelty of riding this new and amazing kind of transport.

The type of hovercraft that were skimming across the waves in the early 1970s was the Saunders-Roe Nautical 6 class, named after the engineering company that developed them on the Isle of Wight, but known as SRN6 for short or *Winchester* class. Weighing six tons (unloaded) or ten tons fully loaded and with a length of slightly under eighteen metres and a beam of eight metres these craft could shoot across the waves at around fifty knots if needed, perfect for a quick journey which would cut the usual travel time by ferry down by a vast amount.

The several hovercraft services running around the UK by 1972 would be ferrying around seven million passengers every year, with usually two operating at any one time to and from the Isle of Wight.

*

Sixty-year-old local man, Reginald Gustaves Hughes, was no stranger to injury after serving in the Second World War. While in the army he was injured at D-Day in 1944, when he was tasked to help recover vehicles that had been left by the side of a path. A booby trapped bomb blew up in the nearby hedge and he was injured badly on his left leg and taken to a hut where he spent 2-3 days in there with other wounded parties. By the time they were able to get him out of the area, the rest of the injured men in the hut were dead, with Reg being the only one left alive. He was sent back to Britain and spent time in Sheffield infirmary with his leg injury, later going closer to home in Cosham to rest and recuperate. The leg would have an open wound which he dressed twice daily for the rest of his life. Despite being in a lot of pain, he hated hospitals and going to doctors and it would be five decades after the war that a doctor asked him about his wound:

'How long has it been like this?'

'Fifty years.'

'I will ask you again, how long has it been like this?'

'Fifty years,' he again replied.

The doctor then turned to Reg's wife Wendy to ask her the same question.

'Fifty years,' was her reply.

The irony is that Reg shouldn't even have been at D-Day. He was a master builder by trade and when war broke out he was busy with building air raid shelters for the Portsmouth area, although forgetting to mention that he was in a reserved occupation, which ended up with him getting his call-up papers to join the army. Later on after the war, on top of his leg injury, he would cut the top of his finger off on a lawnmower!

After the war had ended, he started his own business in 1946, calling himself RG Hughes Builders, and after the war there was a high demand for contractors due to the large amount of bomb damage caused by the relentless raids by German aircraft. No sooner had VE day been celebrated than his business took off with work coming in thick and fast. He was never one to just do his work and then rest, he liked to keep active, regularly taking part in ballroom dancing and swimming. He always had his pet dog, an Alsatian called Trixie, in the back of his pick-up truck; in fact the dog lived in the front seats even at home, refusing to come into the house, being more than happy to lay in the truck.

*

The morning of Saturday 4th March 1972 was a stormy day, with a wind whipping the waters of the Solent up sending spray onto the promenade at Southsea to add to the cold air that was already biting at those walking the streets. The hovercraft services were still running although all eyes were firmly fixed on the weather ready to cancel any crossings should it be classed as too rough in the gale force winds to the point of being dangerous. The last thing anybody wanted was the £140,000 craft being damaged by the storms or worse, causing injuries to their paying passengers.

One of those out that day was fifty-seven-year-old Anne Barbara Robinson who lived a few miles away in the village of Rogate, near Petersfield, and was returning from the Isle of Wight after visiting her sister Rosemary. An active woman she enjoyed playing county tennis and was particularly fond of belly surfing at the beach in Cornwall – there were no wet suits then! Although she never married, Anne was always busy with the likes of her local community. She was a Midhurst Rural and West Sussex County Councilor, well liked in her village, and served on the West Sussex Education and Social Services Committees, was Chairman of the Western Area Social Services Committee and governor of a number of schools in the area. She was also a founding member of the Terwick Housing Association which had just completed nineteen sheltered flats for the elderly in the village. For ten years she was a churchwarden at Rogate and took a great interest in church affairs. She had represented Rogate at three levels of local government – elected to Parish council twenty years previously, Rural Council in 1963 and County Council in 1970, also being leader of the Rogate Girls Club from 1947 to 1957. Needless to say she was well known and well liked in her area.

Seven-year-old schoolgirl Julie O'Connell from Southsea loved the Southsea hovercraft. She was mad about them and had wanted to go on one for a long time. She was doing really well at school, with her two older sisters and mother being very proud of her progress; she had even been taking ballet lessons for the last year in her spare time. She had been promised for a long time an opportunity to travel on the hovercraft by family friend Charles Street, who lived just a few roads away. She was to make the journey across the water on the hovercraft and, as excited as ever, today was the day she would finally go on one. That morning they had both made the journey across to the hover terminal and then gone over to Ryde for the day. Now it was getting late in the afternoon and it was time for them to start making the return journey on that windy afternoon.

6

However, the wind didn't seem to bother the hovercraft pilots. The operating limits for the craft are set by the Air Registration Board, and Hovertravel had already tested their endurance by taken one of their other hovercraft up the River Amazon in winds of up to sixty knots, so today was nothing that the SRN6 couldn't reasonably handle. Passengers paid their 50p for the single ticket (£1 for a return) and waited at the Ryde terminal for a slight repair to be carried out on the skirt. It wouldn't be long until they would be on board and heading for the mainland.

SRN6-012 at Ryde approx 1971.

SRN6-026 which is the same class as the one that capsized.

Inside an SRN6 (stretched) hovercraft on display at the Hovercraft Museum.

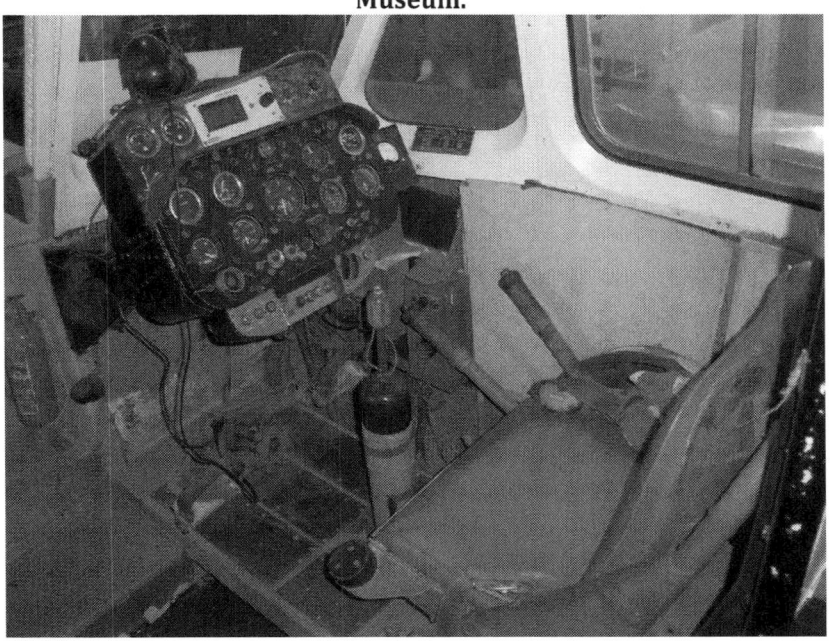

Inside an SRN6 (stretched) hovercraft on display at the Hovercraft Museum.

Above left: Anne Robinson taken in Cornwall approx 1969
Above right: Reg Hughes with his dog Trixie

12

2. Capsize

Early on that Saturday morning, builder Reg Hughes and his friend Frank Goodwin, who both shared an interest in fishing, decided to head over to the Isle of Wight to check out a fishing boat that was for sale belonging to Jack Hargreaves, the fisherman from the TV series 'Out of Town' which was popular at the time. Frank was a carpenter and Reg brought him along to share his knowledge and expertise and to make sure the boat was in good working order, and more to the point if it was worth the money.

When they arrived by hovercraft in Ryde, they made the short journey to where the fishing boat was, liked what they saw and organised the transaction there and then, later renaming the boat *Regus* after himself. Happy with their purchase, that afternoon they headed back to the hover terminal for the return journey to Southsea on the *SRN6-012*, one of five hovercraft owned by Hovertravel. Reg's nephew Mark had been off school ill during the week but really wanted to go over on the hovercraft with them. However, his reply to that was, 'No....if you're ill, you're ill,' and he wouldn't allow him to go.

Frank was a nervous traveller and had never been on a hovercraft. As he entered through the bow door, he remarked, 'How do you get out of this then in an emergency?' and somebody showed him how to use the emergency exit on the windows. It was as if he knew something was going to happen.

As the craft arrived at Ryde at 15:55 it was the normal custom to refuel, but the pilot Anthony Course decided he had sufficient fuel and would prefer to see the small defect in the skirt of the port bow being repaired; what is known as a 'finger', which he had noticed had come off. It was nothing more than general maintenance as it had no effect whatsoever on stability or how the craft operated, it was just good practice to keep the skirt in top condition and for any slight anomaly to be repaired as soon as possible. For those waiting at the terminal, an announcement was made informing passengers that a repair to slight damage would take a few minutes and boarding would commence soon. Sure enough the bow door was swung upwards and passengers began to embark and take their seats.

Course and another pilot would usually take it in turns, 2-3 hours each, to make the crossings; whichever one was left behind would operate the shore radio and be on standby. This crossing, the ninth that day, would be no different to any of the others; Course had already been on duty since early that morning and was the pilot for this run, since 14:50 when he had taken over. A married man, he had joined Hovertravel just two years previously with already several years experience and 2,200 hours piloting their hovercraft, as well as hundreds more with a previous company. No stranger to the sea he had been in the merchant navy since 1956.

With all the passengers safely seated, at 16:03 the craft powered up again, slid into the freezing waters of the Solent and started the four-mile crossing to Southsea carrying twenty-six passengers. Normally this would take around 7-9 minutes but today it seemed he would have to take it steady as winds were now gusting up to fifty knots with waves of up to eight feet.

*

Guy Higgins had already worked for Hovertravel several times, joining in the late 1960s, and at this moment he was working as ground crew, which meant loading and unloading, terminal work and occasionally travelling in the hovercraft itself. That route was undertaken normally by two craft, but today it was *SRN6-012* on its own making approx ten trips, once every hour. The other craft, *SRN6-130,* was back over at Ryde and not being used.

The state of the weather that day could only be described as freak conditions. The sea was quite rough but the craft had been operating the same route in the same conditions all day; Guy had even taken a crossing in the morning and a return trip in the afternoon. He described the crossings as a bit bumpy but with no problems. There was no reason why this crossing would be any different, after all the experienced crews knew what they were doing.

Just after 4pm he was in the beach hut (where the beach master would be) with a minibus driver and a cashier, waiting for *012* to return and preparing for the arrival. As the craft was getting to within the last mile of Southsea he started taking more notice of it as it would now be slowing down. There were very strong tidal currents at that location and the craft started bouncing in the troughs, going up on one wave sideways, then down into a small trough, then the craft went up a second wave, again sideways on, but this time it slid down into a much longer trough. Pilot Anthony Course noticed that he was being pushed to the west of the way he wanted to go by the wind and to a certain extent by the sea.

Because of the angle, the water came in through the port side puff ports; at this point the water could not get out of the skirt and they continued for a brief few seconds to stay at that angle. The pilot had reduced speed from around thirty-five knots down to around ten to fifteen, which is normal procedure for coming into the terminal, but as she got to within 400 yards of Southsea the constant rocking and hitting the troughs of the waves became too much. The craft dove down sideways into a new trough until the whole port side was pointing down at a steep angle. This exact spot was known as Hamilton Banks, a very shallow area of water. The time was 16:11, just eight minutes after the craft had left Ryde and so close to finishing the journey. As the craft rolled over, people started falling out of their seats as spray hit the windows. Looking to the left the passengers could see water, looking across to the right they saw sky. Things were starting to go very badly wrong. The pilot shouted for people to put on lifejackets out of instinct, but it was too late as he was thrown out of his own seat and the ten-ton craft reared up.

The impact of hitting the trough was so severe that it gave the strong winds a chance to catch the underside of the craft and push the starboard side up and literally turn it over onto its side, normally an impossible feat, before flipping the craft completely over. It took just a few seconds to capsize. Guy Higgins, watching from across the water, expected it to right itself and come back down again, but by now the pilot would have had no control over the craft and it would have been impossible to right it. He would describe it going over as 'not so much violent and instant, but more graceful'. It rolled over in a cloud of steam and spray as if 'somebody had pierced a bag of flour' and then settled upside down. If it had recovered from the initial up-ending it would have been okay, but in that small stretch of water it was not to be. The area in between the two channel buoys was around a 200ft-wide area. Watching from the shores the craft seem to flip over in virtual silence. On the craft itself it was a different story as the normal crossing suddenly turned into a major drama.

Course immediately opened the bow door to evacuate the passengers; water flooded in as all around the craft the emergency windows were kicked out. The upturned craft now floated around upside down, drifting in the current away from the hover terminal and down towards the east. People were starting to leave the craft via any means possible although, unknown to everybody, as water was flowing in from every angle several people would be trapped in the overturned wreck.

Guy Higgins couldn't believe it had just happened; a minibus driver was in the hut with him and Guy just said to him, 'My God, she's gone over!' by now realising this was a major incident. He instantly grabbed the phone and rang 999 from the beach hut, whilst watching the drama unfold out of the window. Guy then contacted the main office in Ryde, getting through to one of the pilots….

'There's been an accident at Southsea.'

'What's happened?' was his reply.

It was too far away for anyone at Ryde to see what had actually gone on with any certainty, unless they were specifically watching that craft, so Guy informed them of the situation as he saw it. By now the hover terminal was becoming a buzz of activity, the Operations Manager coming into Ryde where Guy would give him a continuous feed of information as it happened and when he could get it.

*

Barbara Jones was a passenger in a car driving along the seafront road from Clarence Pier eastward on that stormy March afternoon. She looked out towards the Isle of Wight just off the terminal for the Hovercraft because there was a group of people on the beach at that point, also looking out to sea. She wondered what they were all staring at. As she followed their gaze, she saw what looked like a raft on the choppy sea about 100-150 yards away from the beach. 'I learned later that this "raft"

16

was the underside of the overturned Hovercraft. Several people were standing on this "raft" and waving to the beach, obviously trying to summon help,' she would tell the author years after the event. By coincidence, her G.P. Dr. Ian McLachlan was heading to the scene to try to help. She learned later that he was connected with the RNLI and helped in the rescue attempt.

Another eyewitness in the same area was Barbara Nicholas who said, 'It was a traumatic and dramatic experience. It was a terrible day, but my husband and I loved walking in the rain, so we were down by Clarence Pier in the storm. That's when we saw the hovercraft had gone over. There's no way that it should have sailed in that weather. As we walked past, the rescuers were asking people to help pull on the ropes. Me and my husband (Dennis) helped pull on the ropes.'

*

Police officer Ian Clapperton was on duty in the Southsea area heading down to Clarence Pier in his Panda car just after the capsize had happened when he saw the car of John Andrews, the auxiliary coastguard in charge of Eastney, Fort Cumberland. By coincidence he was parked up at Clarence Pier car park watching the hovercraft through binoculars for no reason other than he enjoyed watching the different vessels plying the Solent. As he focused on the *SRN6-012* he saw the craft go over from where he was and had grabbed his car radio system and issued an immediate mayday to the marine rescue centre. Ian then followed suit and radioed to the police control room in Queens Crescent to report the incident; he would then remain at the scene for several hours while the rescue operation was taking place. Looking across at the craft, in his experience and judgement, he expected fatalities with the state of the weather and the unusual nature of the wreck. Out of Portsmouth Harbour came several police motor boats to join the Bembridge lifeboat and several other small boats out of Camber docks, although the two Westland helicopters would most likely be seen to be doing the lion's share of the rescuing; each survivor would be winched up and taken over to Southsea Common where they would be landed one by one to be taken into the care of waiting ambulances.

Over at the Ryde hover terminal, Guy Higgins saw the helicopters from Thorney Island arrive very quickly; because of the quick reaction of the coastguard officer, both were on scene around ten minutes after the initial call. There were many more hours of work to be done, watching the rescue operation unfold, not knowing who was alive and who was missing. It was his job now to help as best he could in this unusual situation. All this time Guy would have the phone line permanently open to feed the HQ at Ryde the latest developments.

*

Meanwhile on the hovercraft itself Reg Hughes had unknowingly saved many lives through Frank's initial query on the emergency escape procedures. As they were nearing Southsea, the craft had barely begun to settle when Frank suddenly leapt out of his seat and began knocking the window out. He was first out and on the top of the upturned craft within seconds. Reg was still on board, his stiff leg causing him problems. Frank bent down and began pulling survivors up onto what was now nothing more than a platform, shouting out 'my boss is down there' to the rescue boats that were now turning up. Moments later Reg managed to get out through the window and when Frank saw him he shouted with joy, 'There he is!'

Trapped in the upturned craft, Reg had tried to move a seat and get out; he saw a child floating and another lady nearby. He lifted the seat off her but it was too late, she was already dead. Remarkably he was saved by the amount of air that was still trapped inside, having to dive down to exit via the same window. Frank noticed that they were now so close to land that he could see the faces of the people now crowded on Southsea beach. The people standing on the upturned hovercraft waiting to be rescued now began to sing 'A life on the Ocean Wave' to keep spirits up. There was no panic; all was calm despite the tragedy unfolding around them. The cold and shock may have been to blame for that as shivering survivors huddled together to await the rescuers.

Diagrams showing capsize

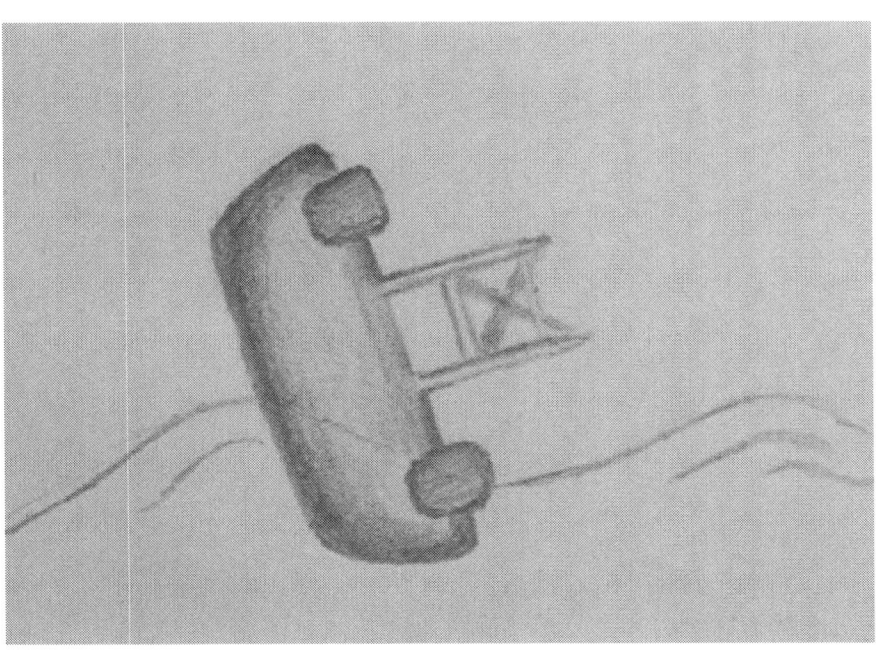

Outline of the hovercraft *SRN6-012*

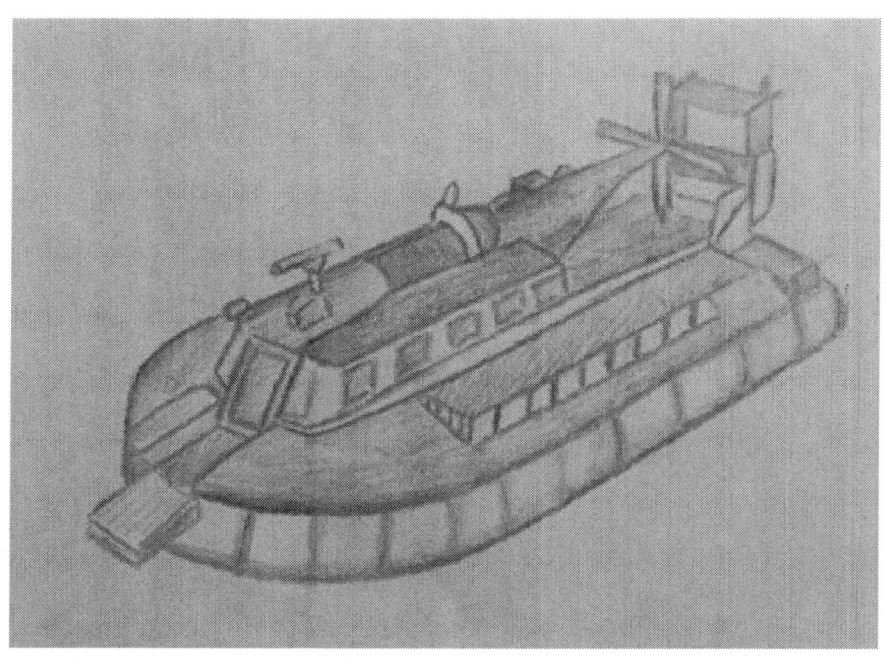

(Diagrams by Jade Convery)

3. The Rescue

Stood on the upturned hull of the hovercraft, pilot Anthony Course counted twenty-one people on top of the craft with him. Nearby he caught sight of a body floating away on its back which he would later identify as passenger David Jones. Looking over to the Southsea terminal, flares could be seen being set off to alert the coastguard and lifeboats in the area. Word was spreading fast and within just a few minutes the first helicopter was on the scene, soon to be joined by a second. The first helicopter took on board five survivors just twenty-two minutes after the capsize, leaving the winch man on the upturned craft to make more space in the helicopter, which then flew the short distance to Clarence Pier to drop the survivors off into waiting ambulances. At the same time a pilot launch came alongside the wreck and took off fourteen adults including Frank Goodwin and a child, before heading to Kings Stairs in Portsmouth Harbour. The last men left on the craft were now the helicopter winch man, the hovercraft pilot Anthony Course and passenger Reg Hughes who couldn't board the boat due to his ongoing leg injury, although he was taken away by helicopter minutes later along with the winch man. Course was handed a lifejacket to wear as he refused to leave his vessel until it was back in Southsea. Reports circulated that knocking could be heard from inside the craft, and there would be no way he would leave while ever there was a chance somebody was still alive down there.

*

As with any major disaster, even those where there is very little loss of life or few injuries, there are moments when normal everyday people become heroes. Lives are put in the balance and it becomes touch and go as to how quickly a human being can go from being perfectly normal to severely injured. The emergency services that Saturday afternoon worked incredibly hard and in complete unison – fire service, police, ambulance, lifeboat, coastguard, harbour tugs, pilot vessels and the armed forces all had roles to play in what happened next.

One of those was Graham Alland, who had started work with the Portsmouth Ambulance Service on 24th January 1966 as a day worker, which meant that it was his job to take all the patients to different clinics and also any of the disabled children to school, the wage then being about £11 a week. Shift work only became available if one of the regular shift men left or passed away and even then it was allocated on a seniority basis, but this was what all of the day men waited for, as it meant more money and a chance to do something a bit more exciting than ferrying people around. So finally after over two years, on the 9th March 1968, it was Graham's turn to be promoted to shift work; now he too would be on a better wage and the real ambulance work would begin. 'Although I don't mind admitting to being somewhat apprehensive of the prospect of some of the severe accidents that the service dealt with and how I would react," he said years later. He had already dealt with two plane crashes at a local airport in Portsmouth which had actually both occurred on the same day, on 15th August 1967.

As news of the hovercraft capsizing raced around the emergency services, ambulances were despatched to Southsea. Graham takes up the story – 'When we arrived the rain was pouring down and it was blowing a gale and at first there was no sign of the Hovercraft, then we saw a helicopter go over and also spotted a small group of people looking out to sea. All we could see from the beach was a group of people some way out to sea near the fort who looked like they were standing on the water (as the hovercraft was flat underneath). We immediately called for back-up and several more ambulances were sent to join us but at the time there was nothing we could do until the helicopters and small craft were able to rescue them and bring them ashore. Southsea Common was right behind us and we knew that would be the obvious place the helicopters would land so we went there and waited. Some of the small craft took the victims into the dockyard and ambulances met them there.

'By this time many more members of the public had started to arrive along with the fire brigade and naval divers. Many little boats were coming out through the harbour entrance and heading for the hovercraft. The first survivors were brought ashore by the helicopters that landed quite close to us, rocking the ambulance with its down draught. We then reversed to the helicopters, but we could not get too close otherwise the blades would have sliced the top off our ambulance.

'Our crew from Portsea Station were the first on the scene and we arrived shortly afterwards from the Eastern Road depot. We spent time arranging things and helped with the loading of the other ambulances that had arrived. It was also not long before Mr Ward, the Chief Ambulance Officer at the time, arrived to take control.'

*

The dog class tug *Setter* was alerted to the incident and it took around fifteen minutes for tug master Jack Clark to get his vessel close to the upturned hovercraft, by which time it was drifting closer to shore and into shallow waters so he was unable to do anything. Around one and a half and three and a half hours after high tide is the strongest tide due to water coming out of Portsmouth Harbour so difficulties were already arising.

One boat, the *Colin Ray*, owned by local firm J Butcher and Sons Ltd was in Camber docks in Portsmouth Harbour when the sound signals were heard going off and news came through that the hovercraft had capsized. Skipper Peter Woolley immediately set off to assist. As he fired up his engine and eased the small boat round past a local bar called the Bridge Tavern he came upon a North Sea diver stood on the jetty who shouted down, 'Hey Pete! Do you want a hand?'

'Yes!' he shouted enthusiastically, backing the boat up allowing him to jump aboard. He then continued the journey, taking the boat round to the entrance to Portsmouth Harbour and, seeing the swell, keeping close to the sides as much as possible. The winds were strong but he was sheltered for now by the walls near the Round Tower, on the way seeing a navy sailor stood near another pub, The Still and West.

The sailor noticed that Woolley and his crew were heading out to sea and shouted down, 'You can't go out there, it's too rough for small boats!' But he was swiftly ignored and the *Colin Ray* proceeded out into the Solent.

As the *Colin Ray* approached the hovercraft wreck they saw that the hover pilot was still standing on the upturned hull with the pilot boat next to her. Woolley shouted out to him, 'Is there anything I can do to help?'

In the gale force winds and noise of the churning sea he was heard to shout back to him, 'Yes, we've lost people over the side, you could have a look to see if you can find any.' Although he didn't say exactly how many they were supposed to be looking for.

The *Setter* meanwhile passed a line to steady the wreck, however the craft started to be pulled underwater with the momentum when it was given any bit of power from the tug, so the line was released leaving the other boat, also owned by Butchers, to keep it in tow alone.

When the *SRN6-012* had capsized, the fuel used, in this case it was kerosene, spilled out into the Solent and left a trail across the water. Following this trail the boat headed across until they came upon what looked like a body near the war memorial not far away. This looked like it was a young girl, but in the rough water it was getting increasingly difficult to recover her with the floorboards on the boat being loose and moving around with the pitch and roll of the vessel. On top of that the crew were becoming increasingly unwell and finding it hard to keep up with the jobs while feeling sick; the North Sea diver being slightly better able to adapt but even he was starting to look ill. However, they managed to recover the girl's body; Peter didn't know much about first aid other than what he had learned when he was in the army but it was obvious that it was too late and she was already dead. With her on board the boat then headed back on the trail where soon they found a large man, so big in fact that they struggled to get him on board. They were forced to leave him attached to the boat via rope until they gathered enough strength to lift him over the side.

Soon one of the helicopters from Thorney Island came in to hover and dropped a winch man down to the *Colin Ray*; he asked if they were all okay. Peter said he was worried about the girl but the winch man just confirmed there was nothing he could do, helping the crew bring the dead man safely on board while he was there. He told them that there was no more searching left to do and to proceed to shore as soon as they could;

the helicopter would radio for an ambulance to be waiting to take their sad cargo from them at Kings Stairs.

It was when the *Colin Ray* entered Portsmouth that the waiting ambulance not only took the two bodies but thought that one of the boat's seasick crew was a survivor and proceeded to put a blanket around him to take him to hospital. The mistake provided a slight bit of humour in an otherwise awful day for all involved.

*

Meanwhile on dry land it was as busy as ever with survivors landing both by helicopter at Southsea Common, and on Kings Stairs on board the pilot launch. At 16:40 Police Superintendent James Sykes arrived just twenty minutes after being alerted to the incident while at home and off duty. He immediately took command of the scene and directed his officers. At the same time ambulances finally began arriving at the Royal Portsmouth Hospital on Commercial Road, the first one carrying six survivors.

Down on Southsea seafront was local taxi driver Eric Robinson who had been in the job for around five years and was working as usual. A lot of the taxi cars had CB radios to talk to each other and as he was proceeding down Osborne Road in Southsea, a call came over his radio from another driver telling him that something was going on at the Southsea seafront, but needless to say nobody had even connected it to a hovercraft, let alone a major freak accident like what had happened. He quickly drove back to see for himself what was going on, and as he made his way to the common he could clearly see the craft upside down. He parked up near where the craft was and proceeded on the main road to where he saw crowds of people hurrying to the scene with equipment to assist in the rescue. He made his way over to the edge of Clarence Pier and looked over at the upside down hovercraft. He witnessed two firemen boarding the craft and continuously attempting to axe the underside of it to make a hole in order to reach the main cabin to search for survivors. He shouted down to them to stop as they would let the air out and it would fill with water and drown anyone left in there. Whether they either heard him or took notice it is not known, but soon Eric was moved away by the police, along with quite a few other people who by now had gathered to see what was happening. The upside down bow was aground on the beach which now sealed the craft's bow door shut. Eric didn't want to see what they would find as it was obvious that nobody could survive for long trapped under that in this weather. He moved out of the way and headed back to his car to continue with his shift.

*

Once she had dropped off her cargo of hovercraft passengers the pilot launch headed back out to sea to continue searching for any more survivors. But with twenty-one passengers in hospital, mostly suffering from shock and exposure, and the pilot about to be taken away, it was evident that no more survivors would be found. The upside down craft had been grounded close to the hover terminal where ropes were attached to steady it. Before 17:00 that evening, less than an hour after the capsize, four bodies would be located: Julie O'Connell and Frederick Street were recovered out at sea by the *Colin Ray*; Anne Robinson was found by helicopter and winched over to Victory Car Park, whereas the fourth, Audrey Jones was found still inside the craft, although at the moment it was too dangerous to recover her. By 18:30 that evening all four bodies had been recovered and were sent by ambulance over to the mortuary for families to begin identification.

In an attempt to re-right the hovercraft an army lorry tried using ropes attached to the craft, but the lines soon snapped and the truck's wheels dug into the shingle on the beach. This attempt was quickly abandoned. As darkness fell, searchlights were rigged so teams could work through the night, but by 20:17 all police units (except one), fire brigade and ambulances were stood down. There was no more rescue work to be done; it was now a case of recovering the wreck.

*

Over at St Mary's City Hospital, morgue worker John Hogan was on watch when the craft capsized and word got through to him that there were sure to be fatalities. Three of the people who died were brought to him that day. Two he described as 'a ten-year-old child with a duffel coat on and a bag of crisps still in her pocket and an elderly lady who had no identification and incredibly no fingerprints'; a police officer telling him that people of the older generation had no washing machines and over the years scrubbed away their fingerprints on a washboard. The third body was what he believed to be the uncle of the little girl, a man in his late forties. John's job was to clean the bodies and pack the people's possessions away for relatives to claim later on. 'You try not to look at the faces,' he would tell the author in 2011.

By Sunday 5th March police had identified Ann Robinson's body, as well as that of the little girl Julie and her family friend Charles Street. However, in the evening there was one body that had still not been identified. She could only be described as a dark-haired woman aged between thirty and forty who had both a wedding and an eternity ring on her finger. She would soon be identified as Audrey Jones, but what shocked police was the information they received when they broke the news to her daughter Caroline who was at home in Surrey. She told police that Audrey was actually with her husband David travelling on the craft and he too hadn't returned home. Investigations found their car parked at the hover terminal. His body was never found although the report of a body floating away by the hovercraft pilot confirmed that he had most likely died in the tragedy and the official death toll was immediately raised to five.

It was reported in the Guardian that Hovertravel could only account for the sale of twenty-five passenger tickets, which would mean there was a twenty-sixth person unaccounted for, out of the living and the dead. The local Portsmouth Evening News reported from police sources that the missing body was trapped inside the hovercraft. This however turned out to amount to nothing. Two women from Cheshire, Ann Atkinson and Jean Dennis, lost all the belongings that they had that day which included their car keys, leaving them temporarily stranded in Portsmouth.

Ambulance man Graham Alland continues his story – 'The hovercraft was eventually towed ashore at Southsea, as it was thought other people could still be trapped inside it. A rope was brought onto the beach, and several sailors, fire and police officers, along with our crews and several members of the public tried to pull the craft onto the beach, but it was hopeless. The fire brigade attacked the flat bottom with axes and oxyacetylene equipment but they were unable to get in, so in the end it was towed in to the dockyard to be lifted over. Five people lost their lives that day; one of them was a young girl that was being taken on a birthday treat by her uncle. I was also somewhat surprised when I got home that evening to find my photograph on the front page of the local evening paper, with the hovercraft pilot.

'A couple of days after this event, I was called into the Chief Ambulance Officer's office and he asked me if I would like to go on an Intubation and Infusion course. This was the forerunner of the paramedic and it was a course that was held in the operating theatres of a local hospital in which you were taught to put up drips and also insert intubation tubes into the unconscious patient, this also meant that we would spend more time at the roadside stabilising a patient before removal to the hospital. You would also spend a week of the course in the casualty department of another hospital and that I found very interesting. As we carried the equipment around with us in a sort of black briefcase, we became known as the "black bag men", and it would amuse some of the patients when they heard a call go out over the radio for a "Black Bag Man".'

*

Guy Higgins stayed on the scene at Ryde until two Hovertravel directors came down from London. He made the journey that late afternoon across the Solent on the company's second hovercraft, the *SRN6-130*, and was put down on the beach about 500 yards from the official hover terminal at Southsea. This journey was full of more senior members of staff going over to the scene of the incident and thankfully there were no problems bringing the craft over in the weather conditions which were still looking pretty bad. Guy took the opportunity to tell the officials about what he had seen and what he had reported to head office throughout the afternoon. Looking around Southsea he saw that the police, fire and ambulance services were all over the area and the whole road by now had been closed off.

Guy located Anthony Course, by now on dry land, and went with him to the hospital. Course was suffering from the cold after spending so much time stood on the upturned craft directing the tow boats and rescuers. He was also suffering from shock, seeming to talk nonsense, he didn't think he recognised Guy, but he still reassured him that everything would be okay as he escorted the pilot to the hospital, which by now had allocated an area especially for survivors. It was decided that Course would be kept in overnight to recover from his ordeal; the company had already contacted his relatives to tell them the news and confirm that he was alive and well.

That night Guy got a taxi back to the hover terminal at about 21:00, staying there until a towing vehicle could start getting the craft moved into Portsmouth Harbour. He left the scene no later than 23:00 that night and stayed in a hotel run by the beach master's friend; it was easier to stay there as it would be hard to travel at this time of night by train to his home in Havant and then back to work early the next day. It had been a long and tiring afternoon for everybody involved.

Course spent the night in the Royal Portsmouth Hospital before returning back to his home on the Isle of Wight the following day. He was photographed by the waiting press leaving the hospital with a large laceration on his forehead. By this time there were only two survivors still being detained, the last one being forty-two-year-old Herbert Self from Alton. A group of photographers had lost all their equipment on board the craft, and two others who had lost everything they had with them were forced to drive back up to their home in the north wearing nothing more than the hospital gowns.

*

As to the family of survivor Reg Hughes, they heard the news breaking at around 6pm that evening when reports came in on radio and television that there had been a 'ferry capsize' off Southsea and gave out an emergency number. Knowing they had been out to the Isle of Wight and had still not returned, Wendy, by now only a week away from her thirty-first birthday, rang the number and asked about Reg and Frank. The reply was shocking: 'Goodwin is here but we can't find Hughes.' Due to Reg and Frank being separated during the rescue it caused a lot of confusion over who was saved and who was alive. Thankfully word got through to them that they had both been saved. Reg had been the last person to be picked up, taken off the capsized craft by helicopter while Frank had been taken by the pilot boat into Portsmouth Harbour. They thought Reg had suffered a broken leg in the accident and they sent him to hospital straight away, but it turned out it was just his old war wound giving him grief as usual. He later remarked that it was not only the first time he had been in a hovercraft and a helicopter, but he had done them both in the same day! At the time of the accident Reg had gone dressed in a three-quarter-length sheepskin coat, and he still had it on when he was recovered from the sea. Being over six feet tall, he realised after a week of the coat drying out that it had shrunk dramatically and wouldn't fit any more.

When Reg had finally got to the hospital he was given a big hug by the nurse to warm him up quickly as they feared he would succumb to hypothermia. He was then taken to the ward with the other survivors and that is where he saw a woman whom he remembered from being on board the craft and having a large black hat. He called to her and said, 'Did you manage to save your hat?' Amazingly, it was there with her under the hospital bed!

Reg did mention to his family that the people from the hover company did not visit any of the survivors nor, he says, did anyone get a refund or compensation, which angered a few of the people involved.

Worse still was what happened when he was discharged from hospital and returned home. Two sisters who were in a dispute with him over some building work decided to send him a nasty letter saying, 'You should have died you old bastard!' This arose when Reg had previously done a job in a ditch on a building site which ended with the ditch being completely filled in and replaced with pipes before being covered over. For some reason these two sisters preferred having a ditch there. They pulled the pipes out and undid all the work the builders had done to the point that in the end Reg had threatened to take them to court for criminal damage. From then on the two sisters ended up running a hate campaign against him.

*

By the following morning it seemed that people had not been put off by the accident; hover services were resumed as normal with the same number of passengers as would be travelling anyway. The general public's trust in Hovertravel to deliver the service safely had not gone away. This was, after all, a tragic accident; a million to one chance. While all eyes and ears were on the investigation that was to follow, the SRN6 class hovercraft still plied the Solent carrying their passengers and would do so until a newer class eventually replaced them in the years to come. It was now down to the engineers and investigators to find out what had happened that fateful day just yards from the safety of Southsea.

The rescue operation is underway as onlookers view the situation from Southsea.

Southsea Common ambulances. (Photo courtesy of Graham Alland and Ron Lilley.)

Above left: The upturned SRN6-012 is towed to shore and beached.
Below left: Hovercraft pilot Anthony Course is led to a waiting ambulance.

4. A question of blame

Immediately following the disaster, the wreck of *SRN6-012* was beached at Southsea upside down, with the fire service still wanting to cut open the bottom to search for any more survivors. By now it was apparent that four people had been killed and one other was missing. However, they soon realised that using cutting tools may ignite the fuel still left in the tanks so they had to wait until salvage crews could raise the craft. Straight away salvage crews would be swinging into action. The aim now was to tow her upside down from her position at Southsea beach across the waters and into Portsmouth Harbour where she would sink to the seabed until a specialist floating crane would lift the wreck up and divers could work on her without the added hazard of the unpredictable waves and currents.

Dave Worsford was one of the divers that day; he had seen the accident all over the news and the morning after the tragedy he and a team got their 36ft dive workboat ready and headed over to the scene. The boat had a metal canopy around 6ft from the bow and left around 3ft at the stern for the helmsman. Dave was the first diver on the rota and entered the water ready to start the grim task of hunting for any further bodies and surveying the wreck. As soon as he could see underneath, it became apparent that the entire top of the craft was crushed flat. Immediately radioing up his report it was decided that in order to carry out any real work of importance the craft had to be lifted completely and turned back upright. Several 'I-beams' had to be placed under the skirt to act as spreaders to prevent any more crushing, which took up the most part of the day. Once the scene was set up and rigged for salvage, the task then fell to the *RFA Swin*, a twenty-eight-year-old Kin class coastal salvage vessel captained by William Thompson. The ship had previously been involved in many huge operations, the most notable being the raising of the submarine *HMS Truculent* which sank in the River Thames estuary in 1950 with the loss of sixty-four sailors.

Tragically the hovercraft accident wasn't the only cause of death at that time. As divers and investigators worked on the hovercraft nearby in Portsmouth Harbour, a diver was killed during work trying to plug a sluice tunnel and was trapped by the suction. Forty-seven-year-old Arthur Howe's body was brought to the surface as several divers engaged in the hover salvage came over to assist. They soon realised there was nothing they could do and went back to the hovercraft salvage. Slowly but surely the craft was turned upright underwater and rigged up ready for the final lift.

On the morning of 7th March, with all eyes focusing on the emerging wreckage, she was slowly lifted from the harbour waters and suspended in mid-air, the weight of the craft causing the stretchers underneath to bend. They had to wait a while until the seawater had drained out of the craft before they could safely lift it onto a waiting barge, as by now it weighed up to twenty-two tons combined and threatened to seriously damage the salvage equipment. The next job was for the police to check inside for human remains and property, but they were concerned about how secure the craft was, and as Dave Worsford was already on it working he was the first choice to go and inspect. However, when it had been towed around the Solent and into the harbour, the rushing seawater had washed clean the craft of everything, leaving nothing more than an empty shell with only its fittings remaining.

The wreck of *SRN6-012* was then lowered gently onto a Royal Navy air lighter for investigators to bring it to the nearest available jetty. Looking at it, it is believed that the craft stayed afloat due to air pockets although it is thought several holes were made by rescuers at the time. This salvage operation had taken all day, most of that time being taken up by the agonisingly slow lifting process. Investigators went inside the craft searching for bodies but found none. It was now time to tow the barge over to the Isle of Wight for the craft to be handed over to her manufacturers who would pore over the remains of the unrecognisable wreck looking for answers. In the last few days many questions had arisen and a lot of them needed answering as soon as possible. While ever there was a danger to passengers the business would suffer and worst of all, it could happen again.

*

The capsizing of the hovercraft shocked not only the hovercraft industry but also the entire country. Never before had such a strange kind of accident occurred. The under secretary of state for Trade and Industry, Mr Anthony Grant, stood up in parliament and made a statement in the House of Commons on Monday 6th March on the disaster. He paid tribute to the victims, expressed sympathy to those bereaved and praised the rescue teams 'without whom the loss of life might have been greater'.

That same day an article in the Daily Express printed a scathing attack on government funding for hovercraft research by the inventor of the craft, Sir Christopher Cockerell. He said that there had only ever been an SRN6 Mark 1 design as there had never been enough money to design a Mark 2. He blamed this lack of funding for the inability to carry out a proper research and development programme. Unlike the aircraft industry, he suggested that 'things start off with a great flourish and then the Government suddenly gets bored with it all'. In his opinion further research could have anticipated such a disaster and the issue have been dealt with before it became a reality, and that he had seen the craft in the Solent in far rougher conditions!

Meanwhile the investigators were hard at work; the police taking statements and engineers working out what had gone so tragically wrong. Officials from Hovertravel worked closely with all parties involved to find out the root cause, and experiments would have to be undertaken. The plan was to carry out tank tests in controlled conditions to learn from the tragedy by using a model of the same class and throwing freak weather conditions at it at different times and at different angles. Only then would they be able to say that what had happened was a one-off event that wouldn't be repeated. Calls to have the landing site at Southsea removed due to its close proximity to Portsmouth Harbour were rejected by Hovertravel, whose immediate response was to restrict all hovercraft travel when wind speeds exceeded thirty knots. This seemed the only sensible option at this time, while the investigation was still being carried out.

*

The inquest into the four people known to have died was opened on the afternoon of 7th March and adjourned until 21st March, eventually hearing evidence on day one, on 19th April 1972, just forty-six days after the accident had happened. The coroner Mr Philip Childs confirmed that there were no defects in the craft and it was perfectly sea/air worthy.

Pilot Anthony Course was praised for the steps he took to help safeguard survivors, highlighting the fact that he stayed with the craft until the last passenger had been winched to safety. The general manager of Hovertravel, Mr Anthony Smith, supported Course's decision to make the final journey in the rough seas saying that the company had made 110,000 Solent crossings carrying 2,250,000 passengers without injury. Before the tragedy there had been forty-two previous cancellations that year because of bad weather. Course had 2,200 hours experience on the SRN6 and had already made several trips that day. He stated that he would have considered cancelling if the wind had been at forty knots and had cut his speed to twenty-five knots which was half his normal speed. Flight Sergeant Stephen Jones from RAF Thorney Island was also praised for the courage shown in staying on the capsized craft so that one more survivor could be taken ashore. At any time he could have been blown off the craft and washed out to sea, the lifejackets having no effect when biting wind and extreme cold were factored in.

In just two days the inquest heard evidence from a total of fifty-eight witnesses which included eyewitnesses, survivors, the pilot and rescuers. Summing up the coroner said: 'It seems to me that it was a well tried design and there is no record of any similar occurrence having happened before. I think you will probably agree that the escape arrangements must be pretty good. Out of twenty-seven persons in that craft, twenty-two survived and they all had to get out from underneath and come to the top.'

The all male jury of ten took just eight minutes to deliver their verdict of misadventure on all five victims. They were named as:–

36

Julie O'Connell, aged 7, of Highland Street, Portsmouth
Mr Charles Street, aged 45, of Lennox Road North, Southsea
Miss Anne Barbara Robinson, aged 58, from Rogate, Sussex
Mrs Audrey Joan Jones, aged 47, from Redhill, Surrey
Mr David Jones, aged 48, also from Redhill, Surrey.

The cause of death for the four bodies which were recovered was officially listed as drowning. The body of David Jones was never found.

*

The official inquiry made the final conclusion on 20th December 1972 that the accident was caused by an unusual combination of circumstances and there was no blame to be attached to the captain, operator or manufacturer. Model tests which were carried out had shown that the strong wind and tides encountered could produce dangerous conditions, but the captain could not have known about it at the time. Urgent investigations into the stability of hovercraft were carried out at the time by the National Physical Laboratory and their results passed to the investigators. After a significantly distressing period for all those involved it was a satisfactory ending to find that nobody was at fault, although lessons would always be learned from such events. The people involved got on with their lives and while the survivors went their separate ways and carried on as normally as they could, the families of those who had been lost that day had to rebuild their shattered lives.

The salvage vessel RFA Swin.

Portsmouth News front page on Monday 6th March 1972.

38

SRN6-012 is brought to the surface inside Portsmouth Harbour.
(Guy Higgins photos.)

Official Police photographs of the wreck on a barge in Portsmouth Harbour. Reproduced by permission of the Hampshire Constabulary History Society.

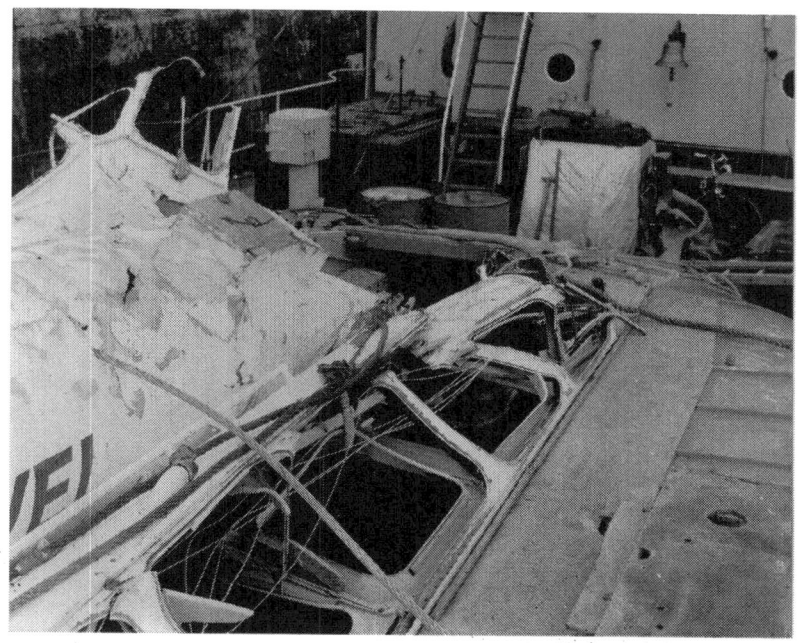

41

Investigators bring the wreckage on shore for analysis.

5. Epilogue

The capsizing of the *SRN6-012* hovercraft would not be the last time that an incident involving such a vessel would make the news. Tragically, several events would darken the record of such a safe way to travel; ironically the worst of these events in question involved the same hovercraft.

There would be two minor incidents involving the SRN6 class before the end of 1972. On 21st October one was involved in a collision off Southsea while on the Ryde route; another collision between a craft and the British Rail ferry *Southsea* caused only slight damage and left passengers shaken. Ironically this left Hovertravel without a hovercraft temporarily as the hovercraft involved in the previous collision was still over in Ryde being repaired.

On Saturday 30th March 1985, the huge cross-channel hover-ferry *Princess Margaret*, an SRN4 mark III owned by Hoverspeed, was making her way past the breakwater at the entrance to Dover Harbour during a storm when returning from Calais. She was carrying 270 passengers, a crew of eighteen and a cargo of thirty cars. In the few minutes it was taking to get the craft from open sea into the safety of the harbour, she suddenly lurched and smashed against the thirty-foot high breakwater. The collision caused a huge gaping hole to be ripped open on her starboard side, killing four of the passengers and injuring thirty-six others. The vessel was taken to the terminal and beached, allowing the remaining passengers to disembark, the injured to be tended to and investigators to go over the craft looking for answers.

This was already the second collision the *Princess Margaret* had suffered; just four years previously on 23rd January 1981 she had done exactly the same at Dover but thankfully everybody got off uninjured. The year previous to that, on 11th October 1980, she had suffered damage by waves and over the years had several instances of skirt and structure damage on her travels. The *Princess Margaret* would be retired from service on 1st October 2000, and both her and her sister craft *Princess*

Anne are now on display at the Hovercraft Museum in Lee-on-Solent, near Portsmouth.

The ship that recovered the wrecked *SRN6-012*, salvage vessel *RFA Swin*, would later be sold and renamed *Francis A Holmes* just two years after her headline mission. On 3rd August 1975, while in the Mediterranean, she suffered an explosion and fire aboard which put an end to her career. She was later taken to Libya to be scrapped but she came adrift from her moorings and grounded, eventually being broken up where she lay.

Survivor Reg Hughes never really went out to sea on his fishing vessel *Regus*, the stress of the hover accident being a bit too much for him, although he did allow friends to go out on it. His eleven-year-old nephew Mark, referring to his leg injury from the war, once jokingly said to him, 'Well they did tell you to soak it in salt water.' The accident did affect him though in many ways. He never really reacted to things before that day, but many years after he would develop heart problems and stress; the cry of the people trapped in the upturned craft would haunt and upset him. He always felt like there was something he could have done even though he knew he couldn't. He would not normally show any emotion and just got on with life as best he could, never really speaking about the accident unless it was brought up in conversation. His friend Frank, at the time living in Warsash with his girlfriend, died of cancer in the early 1980s leaving behind a son and two grandchildren.

Reg's nephew Mark would follow in his footsteps and join him in the building trade, being so pleased that he renamed his company RG and MA Hughes. On 28th August 1991, aged eighty, Reg died, his cremated ashes being scattered in his widow Wendy's garden. He originally left his body to medical science but due to the fact he had to have an autopsy, it was rejected. Mark took over his business and continues to trade to this day.

RAF Thorney Island continued to serve the area well as, among other things, a search and rescue centre, until closing as an air base in 1976. Today it is operated as a base for the Royal Artillery and renamed Baker Barracks.

The wrecked hovercraft *SRN6-012* would later be repaired and renamed *SRN6-055* and sold to a foreign nation. She would eventually be scrapped years later.

The Royal Portsmouth Hospital where all the survivors were taken was closed in 1979 after 130 years service. The building was demolished and today a branch of supermarket chain Sainsbury's sits on that spot.

The small boat *Colin Ray* which recovered two of the bodies of the victims was later sold to a company on the River Hamble where it was renamed and still operates today in the area. The skipper Peter Woolley suffered quite bad post-traumatic stress over the years, being upset that in the back of his mind he maybe could have saved Julie O'Connell's life, that he wrote her off too early, and this thought haunted him for a long time. It would be many years before he would accept that there was nothing he could have done that he didn't already do.

For those involved in the accident, life had to move on as best as it could. The story faded from the news remarkably quickly and today is barely remembered. I did suggest putting up a plaque near to the scene to honour those who died but it seemed that the families of those who died would rather not. With this in mind I ended my campaign and to this day there is no memorial other than this book to commemorate the capsizing of *SRN6-012*.

Today, a hovercraft service still operates from the same company doing the same run. It was only sheer bravery and the skills of the emergency services that prevented an even bigger catastrophe that day. The heroic actions of pilot Anthony Course and the quick rescue of the survivors is something that should never be forgotten.

A later propeller taken from the *SRN6-012* on display at the Hovercraft Museum.

Southsea Hovercraft Terminal today.

<u>Acknowledgments</u>

Hovercraft Museum, Lee-on-Solent
Hampshire Constabulary History Society
Portsmouth News

Graham Alland
Barbara Jones
Eric Robinson
Guy Higgins
John Hogan
Ian Clapperton
John Jenkins
Gustaves Hughes
Edgar Craven
Warwick Jacobs
Dave Worsford
Barbara Nicholas
Stephen Moore
Susan Fowler
Gary Crook
Peter Woolley
Jade Convery

Printed in Great Britain
by Amazon

31668798R00033